Chaos Theory

A collection of poems
by
Robert Hale

a Hitting The Road Again Blues publication

Chaos Theory
A collection of poems by Robert Hale
A Lulu Book

© Robert Hale 2011 All Rights Reserved

Cover Image : Robert Hale, 2011

ISBN: 978-1-4475-9332-4

thehittingtheroadagainblues.blogspot.co.uk
stonesfromtheroad.blogspot.co.uk
aworldlens.blogspot.co.uk

Contents

The Couple
Away From The Crowd
Fields
A Valentine's Day Poem
Mourning Haiku
Traces
The Pig
Three Haiku
The Lost City
The Metaphor Machine
The Death of Silence
Build A Better Mousetrap
Watching
You Are Mister Potatohead
All Things To All Men
From Out Of The Deep
Day By Day
Ten Items Or Less
The Return of the Invisible Fish
The Monster
Birthday
Exhibition
Bird Blind
Watching Clouds
Liberation
Balance
I Wish I Speak Well English
Love Sequence
Teaching Fox To Fly
Transient Poetry
Chaos Theory
Capturing The Thunder
These Were the Ways Of The Ancients
The Chinese Village

Lucky Dip
Balloons
Cave Art
A Christmas Song
The Teddy Bear House
Stars: A Fibonacci Poem
Bounce
Contemplating Suicide
On Being Joined In The Pub By Two Female Colleagues Whose
        Limited Range Of Conversational Gambits Had
        Previously Been Remarked Upon
Dave
Preparing For The Adventure
My Korean Statues
Broken English
Closing Scene

Chaos Theory: A branch of applied mathematics studying systems in which arbitrarily small changes in the initial conditions can lead to extreme changes in the final conditions rendering prediction of the outcomes of such changes impossible.

Seems to me that it's a pretty good definition of life.

The couple

On a sheltered bench on the seafront they sat,
looking out at the sea through the rain.
As I passed them, I gave them a tip of my hat.
I had seen them before and would see them again –
an old woman, her coat buttoned tight to her chin,
an old man with hands folded on top of his cane –
and I asked how they were; they looked fragile and thin.
The old man spoke for both; said, "Mustn't complain."

Away from the crowd

I have walked away from the noise and the fires.
I am sitting alone at the edge of the sea.
I have left them the party, the music, the pyres.
The present is theirs, but the past is for me.
I have seen them and heard them, I know what they say.
They say I'm a killjoy who will not join in.
They think that I think I am better than they.
The truth is that memories are crowding my skin.
A year to the day, the decision was taken,
as I stood in the rain at the side of her grave,
that something inside me now needed to waken;
that I could not find there the things I would crave;
that I'd travel the world and with every new land
hope that my life would have made her feel proud,
but sometimes the sadness overwhelms me still and
I find I must walk away from the crowd.

(For my mother.)

Fields

"I remember when this was open field,"
says my father.
He says that kind of thing a lot.
I listen, boredom ill-concealed.
On the whole, I'd really rather
That he'd not.
These house are not even new.
I've driven past
each day for twenty years,
but suddenly I'm startled by the view
as I realise at last
that now, I remember fields too.

A Valentine's Day poem

I'd like to write a poem
of a love that's deep and true,
that's brighter than the sunshine
and fresher than the dew,
that lasts for all eternity
yet begins each day anew,
adds music to the sounds of life
and grandeur to the view –
and the only thing that's missing
is someone to send it to.

Mourning haiku

The grass overgrown,
apples lying where they fell:
untended garden.

(For my father.)

Traces

The room still bears their traces
surrounding the spaces where they sat:
abandoned books, forgotten pens
notes they will not see again, notes that
they made with half-attentive care,
left scattered there on the final day
jetsam cast away, driftwood on the beach.
There's no one left to teach.
I sigh and start to clear away.

The pig

Under the villager's hut,
between floor and muddy ground,
there is a pig.
We stand in a semi-circle,
and take its picture.
The villagers stand in a semi-circle
and watch us standing in a semi-circle
taking its picture.
An old man smiles proudly.
"In England," he says,
"They do not have such fine pigs.

Three haiku

Children and their dog;
catch-ball choreography
beneath whispering trees.

The pavilion roof;
a comfortable cat watches
children and their dog.

Shaded by reeds
frogs grumble in the water;
park life surrounds them.

The lost city

I used to know each city street;
each path remembered by my feet;
each doorway in its proper place;
each window that contained my face.
I used to know each turn and twist,
could close my eyes and make a list,
of every building, every road.
Their ways became my secret code.
But then, one day, I went away –
did not return until today
and I found I'd paid the cost.
What was my city had been lost.
We met as strangers not as friends
for left untended friendship ends,
and my friend, the city, knew me not;
like me, alone, it just forgot.

The metaphor machine

Pull the lever, press the button,
turn the dial and flip the switch.
The machine begins to work;
it all goes without a hitch.
No one seems to notice
that it doesn't do a thing.
The machine we know as life
has got a broken spring.

The death of silence

There is music in the shops.
There is music in the bars.
There is music on the streets
and there is music in the cars.
There's a soundtrack to our lives
that was never there before,
and music piped into the ears
of those still wanting more.
There is music everywhere
as we go about the day.
Where did the silence go?
When did they take it all away?
And was the silence buried,
unloved and unremarked,
in a graveyard of lost things,
forgotten in the dark?
Does no one miss the silence?
Am I the only one,
that's ever even noticed,
that the silence has all gone?

Build a better mousetrap

To build a better mousetrap...

Darken the eyes;
Redden the lips;
Uncover the thighs;
Gyrate the hips.

To build a better mousetrap...

On with the paint;
On with the show;
Out with restraint;
Never say no.

To build a better mousetrap...

Go find the mice;
Offer the bait;
Attract and entice;
No need to wait.

As the mice take the cheese.

Watching

Watching the diamonds
dance in the water;
remembering moments
before your goodbye.
You said the sunlight
was trapped by the water
and couldn't escape
to get back to the sky.

Watching the ghost dance
of rippling leaves;
remembering moments
when you were here.
You said the voices
of whispering leaves
were the souls of dead lovers
trapped in this sphere.

Watching the cloudscapes
built high in the blue;
remembering moments
before you were gone.
You said the unborn
inhabit the blue
and the clouds were the islands
they built their homes on.

Watching the shadows
creep through the gravestones;
remembering moments
when I thought you'd stay.
You said the shadows
cast on the gravestones
were memories slowly,
but surely, draining away.

You are Mister Potatohead

Rearrange the features to make another face.
Fix the plastic smile firmly in its place.
Choose the ears and eyes; choose the mouth and nose.
Choose the shape and size and where all of it goes.
And when the thing is done, join the others in the game,
secure in the knowledge that they've all done the same.

All things to all men

He's the picture of the Everyman;
his talents know no end;
his popularity is limitless;
he's everybody's friend.

Nine to five, five days a week,
he teaches in a school.
His colleagues think him erudite;
his pupils say he's cool.

He often spends his evenings
down in the pub with mates
who've known him since their schooldays
and they all think he's great.

He's a font of funny stories -
tales both coarse and clean.
Call him erudite or cool
and they won't know what you mean.

His parents and his siblings
think of him as shy,
as reticent at best,
as a bird who'll never fly.

On the terraces on Saturdays
he's with a cruder crowd
but blends right in by being
both partisan and loud.

When he goes on holiday,
he's a traveller and more,
with tales of all the countries
that he's visited before.

The neighbours in his street
all say, "A quiet chap -
never causes any fuss,
never gets into a flap."

A description that is chilling,
for therein lies the clue
to this chameleon's nature,
to the colours that are true.

The way that he is seen,
by the servants of the law,
is formed by what was buried
beneath his kitchen floor.

From out of the deep

She is old now but she remembers in new ways,
so her days are filled with the jumble of the past.
Nothing lasts. Nothing is in its proper place.
She sees faces she recognizes, and smiles,
in the supermarket aisles, but no one smiles back.
Her history is packed into her head like a jigsaw;
but before it's taken from the box. Just pieces,
it ceases to have a shape for her, a form.
Instead a snowstorm of randomness blinds her
and little things remind her of days long past.
As she casts her eye upon the city's sweep,
From out of the deep, she catches a summer day,
and, momentarily, she plays again in sunshine,
aged nine. The depths give back their gold.

Day by day

Day by endless passing day,
we give portions of ourselves away,
become old and sad and grey;
day by endless passing day.

Day be endless passing day,
we forget the things we meant to say,
change from predator to prey
day by endless passing day.

And day by endless passing day,
we allow our essence to decay,
until, invisible, we pray
this is the final passing day.

Ten items or less

One box of childhood memories in assorted flavours,
one pair of school plays: a wise man and a knave,
one tin of condensed education,
one bottle of sweet and sour first love,
one kilo of mathematics, left in the back of the fridge,
one six pack of early jobs,
one jar of pickled travel,
one microwaveable life for one,
one tube of regrets, squeezed out slowly,
one disinfectant block of dissolving possibilities.
Checkout!

The return of the invisible fish

Look, there in the tank.
Look, there by the bubbles.
If you look closely, then you will see
the hint of a spine
and a motionless hole,
shaped like a fish, where a fish ought to be.
And there in that hole,
there in that space,
look closer for traces of what's hiding there.
Could that be an eye?
Could that be a heart?
An invisible fish? Well, I declare!
There in the corner!
And there by the castle!
And under the rocks, in the shade of that hole!
Could that be another?
Another? Another?
The aquarium's full, an invisible shoal.
"But why," asks the child
"Have invisible fish?
Surely a goldfish is better to own.
What is the point
If no one can see them?"
"You'll understand better," I say, "When you're grown."

The monster

"There isn't a monster under the bed!"
That's what my mother always said.
"There isn't a monster under the bed!"
But what do mothers know?

"Of course there's a monster under the bed!"
That's what my brother always said.
"Of course there's a monster under the bed,
And he's nibbling on your toe."

"There might be a monster under the bed."
That's what my father always said.
"There might be a monster under the bed
Who wants to be your friend."

"It's a terrible monster under the bed."
That's what my brother always said.
"Such a terrible monster under the bed.
He'll eat you end to end."

"There isn't a monster under the bed!"
Lying awake, that's what I said.
"There isn't a monster under the bed."
But I knew I didn't believe.

"Of course there's a monster under the bed!"
From under the bed, the monster said.
"Of course there's a monster under the bed
And I have no plans to leave."

The birthday

He went and bought a birthday card
and sent it to himself,
and when the postman brought it,
he put it on the shelf.

He wrapped himself a birthday gift
and tied it with a bow.
He feigned delight on opening
and cried, "How did you know?"

He baked himself a birthday cake,
for each year lit a candle,
and made the wish he always made
to lead a life of scandal.

He sang himself a birthday song
and finished with a cheer.
He opened up the fridge, then sat
and drank a can of beer.

He gave himself the birthday bumps -
the task was rather vexed
but tradition is tradition and
the bumps were what came next.

He allowed himself a birthday treat
and stayed up rather late,
played Windows hearts and solitaire
and whispered, "Ain't life great!"

Exhibition

Tracy Emin sewed a tent
with every lover's name.
I'm not suspicious-minded but,
when it went up in flame,
I couldn't help but wonder which
of them should take the blame.

Rachel Whiteread had a house.
She turned it inside out
by filling up with concrete mix -
a prize winner no doubt,
that had the added benifit
of keeping burglars out.

Paintings made with added dung -
the work of Chris Ofilli,
and some among the critics yawned
proclaiming it too silly.
But they will burn like billy-o
if the weather should turn chilly.

Damien Hurst displayed a cow
he'd cut up with a knife
and in the world of art today
that kind of thing is rife.
It would have been a better trick
to bring it back to life.

Mark Wallinger, he walked around
a gallery at night.
To make sure he was seen there
he turned on every light
and dressed up as a bear.
Some said, "That bloke's not right."

Martin Creed turned off the lights
and then he turned them on.
Then off, then on, then off, then on.
Some said it was a con.
And when he left them on, at last,
his audience was gone.

(For what it's worth, I am personally rather fond of conceptual art. These nursery rhymes should in no way be taken as a reflection of my own views.)

Bird-blind

I can't tell a wren from an emu.
I can't tell a finch from a quail.
Ask me to point out a penguin.
there's a pretty good chance that I'll fail.

I think what we have is a budgie,
'cause a turkey won't fit in a cage,
but hoopoe and heron and hornbill
are pictures and words on a page.

At Christmas I recognize robins,
on a card with some holly and snow,
but outside on a branch or in flight
could be vultures for all that I know.

If you point at the sky, my eyes follow
and I look at the circling dot,
but is it a swift or a swallow?
or a Dodo? (Well probably not.)

A condor, a jackdaw, a lapwing,
a pelican, puffin or kite,
a woodpecker, ptarmigan, eagle
are all just the same in my sight.

Believe it or not, I am bird blind.
I'm not ornithologically graced,
but it's not all bad news, I can tell
A duck from a chicken... by taste.

Watching clouds

She said, "The clouds look like rabbits."
I agreed but I was lying,
The clouds looked like clouds.
She said, "The clouds look like dragons."
I agreed but I was lying,
The clouds looked like clouds.
She said, "The clouds look like angels."
I agreed but I was lying,
The clouds looked like clouds.
She said, "The clouds look like faces."
I agreed but I was lying,
The clouds looked like clouds.
I said, "The clouds look like clouds."
And now when I watch the clouds,
I watch them alone.

Balance

I'm watching the news,
but on closer inspection,
I can't help believing
it's all misdirection.
The words and the images
that flash on my screen
mean no more and no less
than they want them to mean.
Like the book of the month,
it's the editor's choice.
I can listen forever
but there's only one voice.
An illusion of balance
is all just a trick.
It makes no real difference
which viewpoint you pick.
I don't know what's true
there's no way to find out.
And that's what control
is really about.

Liberation

"It's been a great success," they said,
"One hundred thousand people dead.
The ones remaining must see how
things are so much better now.
Why do we meet with so much hate,
From those we want to liberate?"

I wish I speak well English

I wish I speak well English.
I wish people not laugh to me.
I wish things like before
when I am important woman.
Not rich. Not rich woman
But have own business.
I dressmaking lady.
I wish soldiers never come.
Now I nothing.
Now I living like nothing.
Like no one.
I wish I speak well English.
I wish much... lots of things.
I wish knowing where children are now,
Where my husband.
I wish I know alive.
I wish they safe.
I wish they here.
I wish I speak well English.

(Poems should always be able to stand alone, without explanation or guidance from the poet. However I feel that it's important to understand the background to "*I wish I speak well English*". I have taught English to refugees and asylum seekers for many years. Their stories are often heartbreaking. Periodically the Government has tried to reduce their rights to English courses while simultaneously complaining that they don't make enough efforts to learn the language. During one of these reductions in provision I attended a protest meeting. Many students also attended and this is a slightly rearranged version of the comments of one student who was crying throughout the meeting because her course, almost her sole remaining human contact, was about to be taken away from her.)

Love sequence

0
0.1
0.2
0.3
0.4
0.5
0.6
0.7
0.8
0.9
0.99
0.999
0.9999
0.99999
0.999999
0

Teaching Fox to fly

raven said:
the trick is this,
do not think of the cliff
think only of the air
fox said:
the cliff looks very high

raven said:
the trick is this,
do not think of the ground
think only of the sky
fox said:
the ground looks very hard

raven said:
the trick is this,
do not think of the rocks
think only of the clouds
fox said:
the rocks look very sharp

raven said:
the trick is this,
do not think of falling
think only of flying
fox said nothing

Transient poetry

on the road
late at night
coming home
having drunk
i make poetry in my mind
i select words from storage
i join them into silent stanzas
i build them into unspoken verse
on the road
late at night
coming home
having drunk
i make poetry in my mind
arriving home
it is forgotten

Chaos Theory

The smallest of lies betrays
the greatest of truths.
Moments too short to measure
lead to eternities of loss.
And this is chaos theory.

I remember her in the crowded airport
hiking boots and a sense of searching
a look on her face
dream dream dreaming of another life.

I remember her in the mountain village
with rain running down her cheeks
across shoulders, down arms
drip drip dripping from fragile fingertips.

I remember her afraid of the ocean
trying to learn as I tried to teach
how to be straw not stone
float float floating, tied to the surface.

I remember her at the hidden beach
worrying about abandoned bicycles
at the head of the trail
fret feet fretting that they would be gone.

I remember her on the castle walls
not silent but strangely sorrowful
wearing a long black coat
look look looking at the cold horizon.

I remember her in the crowded airport
misleading tears on her pale skin,
tears at parting, she said
dream dream dreaming of another life.

The smallest of lies betrays
the greatest of truths.
Moments too short to measure
lead to eternities of loss.
And this is chaos theory.

(For A.)

capturing the thunder

some would capture the lightning
hold it in a globe
bring it into the darkness
and free it to illuminate the world
from light comes peace

but i would capture the thunder
hold it in a box
bring it into the silence
and free it to create chaos and confusion
from sound comes change

These were the ways of the ancients

These were the ways of the ancients
-----they built cities to gather the people
-----and walls and fences to separate them;
-----they lived all together and all alone

These were the ways of the ancients
-----they accumulated tokens of wealth
-----mistaking them for tokens of worth;
-----consumed by their consumerism

These were the ways of the ancients
-----some chose their dictators by ballot
-----some allowed their dictators to choose them;
-----all followed their dictators dictats

These were the ways of the ancients
-----they worshipped strange disparate gods
-----and mocked each others' stranger pieties;
-----all would be saved and all damned

These were the ways of the ancients
-----they filled their lives with sound and light
-----their bodies with alcohol and drugs;
-----they were stimulated and stupefied

These were the ways of the ancients
-----they reached for peace by waging war
-----measured success by counting corpses;
-----their passions were primitive, they were not us

The Chinese village

I was alien,
a pale specimen skewered;
silent winter eyes.

Lucky dip

policeman, politician, programmer or pilot
divorced or married, widowed, all alone
playboy millionaire or a shy and shrinking violet
philanthropist or heart as cold as stone

morose or happy, sorrowful or overcome with joy
famous or forgotten, a sinner or a saint
a good life or a bad life; build, maintain, destroy

take a ticket from the lucky dip; accept without complaint

Balloons

How easily they have broken the chains
that tied them to the shattered ground;
slipped free of grasping gravity;
left the yellow Earth
to skim the tops of scrubby trees.
Each takes its brighter shade
away to the hills.
They diminish until nothing remains
but the memory of them all around.
Silence pours now into the cavity
into the void, into the dearth
where they vanished by degrees.
As I watched their airy presence fade,
I felt the morning chills.

Cave art

It's all only art on the walls of a cave,
messages sent from a cold ancient grave;
down through the ages in primitive shapes
histories passed on from apes unto apes.
These words that I write, they are more of the same,
I am one of the ones who is passing the flame
by drawing my art on the walls of the cave
and sending it forth, beyond life, beyond grave.

A Christmas song

Waking up on Christmas Eve,
Danny made a cup of tea,
placed the gift he'd bought himself
beneath his plastic Christmas Tree.
In the mirror on the wall,
said "Merry Christmas" to himself,
left the sprig of mistletoe
wrapped in paper on the shelf.

On the streets the snow was falling.
Danny left his two roomed flat,
took the tube into the city,
in the subway saw a rat.
Oxford Street was filled with people.
Neon angels watched on high.
Danny only killing time,
had no presents he should buy.

He saw families all together.
He saw lovers arm in arm.
He saw himself in shop windows,
saw his face a mask of calm.
How he hated Christmas time,
more than any other day.
Everyone was busy joining
in a game he could not play.

He went into a crowded bar
to try to find some Christmas cheer,
spoke to no-one but the barman,
stood alone and drank his beer.
On the street the light was fading,
shop window beacons shone around.
The Neon Angels were still watching
the hordes that walked upon the ground.

Standing high on Vauxhall Bridge,
the snow now turned to sleet and rain.
Danny watched the Thames dark waters
promising an end to pain
He climbed the rail and spread his arms,
yelled "Merry Christmas !" to the sky
and as he fell towards the river
in his mind he'd learned to fly.

The Teddy Bear House

There are bears on the stairs.
 There are bears in the chairs.
There are bears everywhere, there are bears.
There are bears in fancy dresses.
There are bears with golden tresses.
In unbearable excesses, there are bears.

There's a bear dressed as a soldier,
a six foot bear whose arms enfold ya
in a friendly, velvet-pawed, bear hug embrace.
There are bears in frilly knickers,
doctor bears and nurses, vicars
and a policeman bear whose bearly on the case.

There are lady bears and gentlemen,
a poet bear with book and pen,
a Bo-Peep bear with more bears in her flock.
There's a bear dressed as a rabbit
and another in nuns' habit.
There's a pointy eared though ursine Mr. Spock.

In the bathroom I am certain
around the shower there'll be a curtain
that's printed with a bear in silhouette
and from the tap hung on elastic
will be a bear made out of plastic
presumably because it might get wet.

A singing bear has tenor warbles
that disturb the bear-shaped baubles
that are strung across the windows and the door.
The cups and plates have bear motif
and it's my firmly held belief
that if I pulled up the floorboards there'd be more.

Wallpaper, carpets pictures,
all the fittings, all the fixtures -
there's nothing in the house without a bear.
The boot and shoe mudscraper,
the thing that holds the toilet paper -
look closely and you'll also find them there.

There are bears on the stairs.
There are bears in the chairs.
There are bears everywhere, there are bears.
In the halls and on the landing,
Bears are seated, kneeling, standing
Other species notwithstanding, there are bears.

(The Teddy Bear House is a real B&B in Alaska.)

Stars: A fibonacci poem

a
star
two stars
and then three
more stars, ever more
until the sky begins to burst

but then the light of dawn arrives
to drive off these sparks
replace them
with one
new
fire

Bounce

I thought I heard a screaming sound,
as I fell towards the ground,
a bungee rope was fastened to my feet.
What, I wondered, could it be?
Then I thought, "Oh God, it's me!"
What a bloody stupid kind of birthday treat.

Contemplating suicide

I will do it in the summer time
when the ground is scorched;
when the blood-hot passion is in every face,
reflected in every pane;
when the lethargic envy burns my thoughts
and a different passion makes my blood race
than that which they entertain

I will do it in the autumn time
in the time of dying;
when the red-gold funeral shroud is cast
over the corpse of summer;
when the pallor of remembrance is lying
tainting the future with the poisoned past
and my heart grows number.

I will do it in the winter time
when the nights grow long;
when the ice-clean cold of dead eternity
swallows the frozen land;
when the pull of the grave becomes too strong
and I hear the call of that fraternity
the great, uncounted damned.

I will do it in the spring time
when all the world's agleam
with life-force green in its newest brightest shade;
when everyone rejoices.
I will make an ironic contrapuntal theme
to this optimistic opera that is played
disregarding other voices.

On being joined in the pub by two female colleagues whose limited range of conversational gambits had previously been remarked upon

I'd have really loved to talk
to someone about something
and I thought, before they entered,
that I didn't much care what.
When they sat down and joined me
I found their conversation
was on topics they found jolly:
and topics I did not.
They talked of shoes and make up
and of bras that didn't fit.
They talked in endless detail
about their clothes and hair,
But things got worse than that
when the topic of the chatter
turned round to the barman
whose bottom made them stare.
There was colonic irrigation,
beauty treatments, oral sex
and what to do with boyfriends
come to visit for the day.
One turned to me and said,
"I forgot you're not a girl, Bob!"
but it didn't stop her finding
lots of similar things to say.
So I finished up my beer,
said, "I don't think there is much
I can contribute to this, or
any other conversation.
So, if it's all the same to you
though it's early, I'll be going."
There's a lot to say for silence
in that kind of situation.

(For K. and A.)

Dave

Every pub from John O'Groats
right down to Land's End,
has inside from time to time
a man who has no friends.
He's always rather scruffy
and he always needs a shave,
he's constantly unwelcome
and his name is always Dave.
He'll introduce himself to you
and join you uninvited
with a sinister and gap-toothed smile
that says he knows you'll be delighted
to have the pleasure of his company
as you sit quietly with your drink
While you are together
he will tell you what he thinks
about everything he's ever seen
and everything he feels.
His converstaions varies
from random to surreal.
He'll talk the hind legs off a donkey
on subjects as diverse
as football, gynacology
history and blank verse.
You can try your best to sneak away
when he buys another beer
but he'll be waiting at the door
and won't let you out of here.
By half past ten he has become,
at least in his own mind,
your bestest mate in all the world
one of his own kind.

Maybe there is just one Dave
who moves from place to place
or an army of the buggers
a sub-species of the race
but if people fail to catch your eye
and never to seem to crave
your wonderful companionship
it might be that you're the Dave.

Preparing for the adventure

I make a list headed
"Things That I'll Need".
Biscuits, chocolate, crisps, more crisps
and squash to wash down the feed.
I'll be wanting a torch
and rope and a spade,
and a bag to hold all these
odds and sods for the plan that I've made.
I catch the bus to the woods
climb over the fence

by the "No trespassing" sign

crossing the line that doesn't make sense.
I sit and I eat
and I wait for my prey
But the forest is empty.
I sigh , and I rise to call it a day
Then from the thicket
A rabbit runs past
Quickly I follow to
its home in a hole - on my way at last.
I take out my spade

and dig all around
I'm going to join Alice
Adventuring deep underground.

My Korean statues

Day after day they sat,
my Korean statues,
silent unmoving, inscrutable -
in , but not of, the class.
Grammar failed to move
my Korean statues.
Vocabulary proved unable
to lift them from their groove.

I tried everything to engage
my Korean statues
to rouse in them a love of lessons
to tempt them from their cage,
but nothing did the trick
with my Korean statues.
They sat through every session
unresponsive as a brick.

They reached the final day,
my Korean statues
with no indication that they'd heard
a word I'd had to say.
Together then they came to me
my Korean statues
and on a card had put the words
"Your lessons make us happy."

Broken English

Everyone agreed. He was an orator of rare skill.
Neither politician nor preacher,
no shaper of men's hearts or minds,
He was rather a public house teller-of –tales,
a bonhomie raconteur, a fine fellow.
His in-his-cups anecdotes enthralled their will
as surely as any teacher
as he weaved stories of a dozen kinds
to an audience who paid with ales
and comradeship, and a grand "Hello!"

But one day he discovered his English was broken.
He reached for a word and found it gone.
Recovering, he went on with his tale
but was shaken by the unaccustomed absence
unnoticed by any there save he himself.
Each day from them as each new thing was spoken
he found more words missing, but struggled on
until, at last, he heard himself falter, fail.
His mind now seemed trapped behind a fence,
or out of reach, placed on some inaccessible shelf.

Everyone agreed. He had been an orator of rare skill,
until the silence had descended
and time and age had stolen all his words;
reduced him to sitting, drinking, remembering stories
that he no longer had the skill to tell.
though in his mind he lived them still.
The days of communication now had ended.
No more were his famous stories heard.
He was now a fellow of former glories,
and eventually a new, and more terrible silence fell.

Closing scene

The boy is standing on the bridge
that crosses the narrowest part
of the stream.
The shot is in a tight close up,
only his face and the leafy
background seen.
He looks sad, but accepting –
a melancholy summer rain
expression.
The camera moves slowly away
teasing details with steady
progression.
It reveals the bridge, the stream,
reveals path upon the shore
and the girl.
The music which was quiet, soft
builds to a mournful crescendo
fills the world.
The camera stops, lingers on
this voyeur's view of sorrow.
She walks away.
The frame freezes to this moment
The credits start to roll.
Fade to grey.

www.ingramcontent.com/pod-product-compliance
Lightning Source LLC
Chambersburg PA
CBHW061251040426
42444CB00010B/2352